INTERESTING FACTS FOR SMART KIDS

1,000+ Random and Fun Facts for Curious Kids

Cooper the Pooper

TABLE OF CONTENTS

INTRODUCTION

Do you like fun facts?

What sort of facts?

Well, things like that the heart of a shrimp is in its head? Or that elephants are the only animal on the planet that can't jump?

Or that turkeys were once worshipped like gods by the ancient Mayans?

I think they should have worshipped dogs to be honest…

But anyway, if you like reading random facts like these, I have got you covered.

See, in your hand you hold one of my best pieces of work.

You have a book that is filled to the brim with over 1000 facts about the world around you. Some of these facts will have you shaking your head in disbelief. Some will have you rolling around on the floor laughing.

Heck, some will even have you questioning everything you thought you knew about the world you live in.

And it is going to be a whole lot of fun – trust me.

See, not so long ago, I spent all my time playing in the sun, digging through the trash, and running around with the neighborhood kids.

But then something happened, and rather than play with *me*, the neighborhood kids began spending all their time with their eyes glued to the TV.

Did someone say *boring*?

So, I decided to make a change. I put on my thinking cap and started brainstorming ways that kids just like you can have *real* fun with your friends and family.

And what better way than with hilarious facts.

As a result, I went on a journey to find the most amazing random facts from around the globe. Then, once found them all, I jammed them into this fantastic book.

Yep, the same book you hold in your hand.

Get ready to laugh, cry, and shake your head uncontrollably – because a world of amazing facts awaits.

01 It is impossible to **lick** your own **elbow**. No one can! Go on and try it.

02 **Rubber bands** break easily, but not if you put them in the **fridge**!

03 You can **fall asleep** in seven minutes; most people do.

04 A **sponge** can hold more **cold water** than it can hold hot water.

05 **Giraffes** cannot swim.

06 Only 11% of people on the planet are **left-handed**.

07 The letter that is **used most** in the alphabet is the **letter "E."**

08 The safest color for a **car** is **white**.

09 The most played board game in the world is **Monopoly**.

10 The item that most people who **travel** always **forget** is their **toothbrush**.

11 Eating an **apple** in the **morning** wakes you up better than drinking coffee does.

12 **Buttermilk** does not actually contain any actual butter.

13 A **giraffe** and a **rat** can survive longer **without water** than a camel can.

14 Statistically, women **blink** at least twice as much as men do.

15 The **hardest** natural substance is a **diamond**.

16 People originally played **tennis** using their **bare hands** instead of a racket to hit the ball.

17 You can only **fold** a piece of **paper** seven times.

18 The first **English dictionary** in history was written in the year 1755.

19 **Christmas trees** were originally from **Germany**.

20 A **gorilla sleeps** for about 14 hours a day.

21 A **butterfly** will drink the **tears of a turtle** if they need salt.

22 The most bought **ice cream** flavor in America is **vanilla**.

23 The **pea** is the **oldest vegetable** that we know of.

24 **Hens** lay around 228 **eggs** a year.

25 The Statue of **Liberty's crown** has seven points.

26 If a month starts on a **Sunday**, it will contain **Friday the 13th**.

27 The part of your **eye** that contains **color** is called an "**iris**."

28 **Moths** do **not have stomachs**, and therefore, they mostly drink liquids such as **nectar**.

29 The most common **allergy** in the world is **cow's milk**.

30 There are 22 **bones** in just your **head**.

31 An **African elephant** only has four **teeth**.

32 The **United States flag** has 13 **stripes** that represent the 13 original states.

33 There is zero **fat** in **carrots**.

34 **Soccer** is the **most popular sport** that is played.

35 **Hippopotamuses** are born underwater.

36 **Elephants** can hold more than five liters of water in their **trunks**.

37 Your **thigh bone** is stronger than concrete.

38 **Sharks' teeth** are actually harder than steel.

39 A **grasshopper's blood** is in fact white, not red.

40 **Bulls** are able to **run** faster uphill than they can run downhill.

41 **Dogs sweat** through their **feet** and their **tongues**.

42 The **song** that is sung the most is **"Happy Birthday."**

43 The **board game of checkers** is older than the board game of chess.

44 A **blonde beard** will **grow faster** than a dark-colored beard.

45 **Squirrels** can live for up to nine years.

46 **Albert Einstein**, a well-known physicist, was known to have **slept** for ten hours a day.

47 A **housefly** only lives for about ten to 25 days.

48 The word **"racecar"** can be **spelled** the same backward as it is forward.

49 **Chihuahuas** are the **smallest dogs** in the whole world.

50 The **teabag** was only invented in 1908; before then, people only used tea leaves.

51 A **snail** can go to **sleep** for up to three years.

52 It takes two hours to **hard boil** an **ostrich egg**.

53 The first country to use **postage stamps** was **Britain**.

54 The name for the **side of a hammer** is **"cheek."**

55 People hurt their thumbs while playing **ten-pin bowling** more than they do any other part of their body.

56 The name **Pinocchio** means **"pine eyes"** in Italian.

57 You should **shuffle a deck of cards** at least seven times before playing with them.

58 **Tooth decay** is the most common disease.

59 **Insects** will **bite your foot** more often than any other part of your body.

60 Our **sun** is about 330,330 times larger than the planet Earth.

61 The **shell of an egg** only makes up for 12% of its weight.

62 A **squid** has a total of ten **tentacles**.

63 A **windy day** is when you are more likely to be **stung by a bee** than any other day.

64 A **woman's heart** will beat **faster** than a man's heart.

65 You have over 10,000 **taste buds** living in your mouth.

66 You **breathe in more air** through your **right lung** than through your left lung.

67 "**Screeched**" is the **longest one-syllable word** in the English language.

68 A **snake cannot blink** at all.

69 **Ants** hate baby powder.

70 A **rat** can **swim** in water for up to three days before getting tired.

71 **Rice paper** does not actually contain any rice.

72 **Sharks** can never stop **moving**, even when they are asleep.

73 Cows will produce more **milk** while they are listening to **music**.

74 A **blue whale** can survive for six months **without eating** any food.

75 A **house cat** will usually have up to 18 **claws**.

76 There are 20,000 species of **bees**, but only four of them can produce honey.

77 **"Save A Spider Day"** is on March 14th.

78 **Avocados** and **tomatoes** are indeed **fruits**, not vegetables.

79 The **Queen of England** has two **birthdays**.

80 Unless you have a twin, nobody smells like you. You have your very own **unique smell**.

81 The **number four** is the only number with the same number of **letters** used to write it.

82 A **slug** has four **noses.**

83 **Hippopotamuses** can **run** faster than humans.

84 An **apple** is one of the few fruits that **float on water**.

85 You **cannot inhale or exhale** while you are **talking**.

86 The board game **Monopoly** has been played by more than 480 million people.

87 It is impossible to **hum** while holding your **nose closed**.

88 Your **fist** is about the same size as your **heart**.

89 There are not any **English words** that **rhyme** with the word "**orange**."

90 **Disney World**, an amusement park in Florida, is actually bigger than about 17 countries in the world.

91 A **yawn** will last for an average of about six seconds.

92 The first **toothbrush** in history was made and used in the year 1498.

93 A **strand of** your **hair** can live for an average of approximately four to seven years.

94 Only the **male toads croak**; female toads do not.

95 **Starfish** do not have a **brain**.

96 **Bananas** are the **most eaten** fruit in **America**.

97 You **cannot dream of strangers.** The people you see in your dreams are people that you have met once before in your life.

98 A **bee** has **four wings**, and it can beat them about **200 times per second**.

99 Your **brain** only makes up 5% of your body's total **weight**.

100 The **elevator** was **invented** as early as 1850 by a man named Elisha Graves Otis.

THINGS YOU
DID NOT KNOW
About
SPACE

01 In **outer space**, you get a **little taller** due to the **lack of gravity**.

02 There is **no atmosphere in space**. This is why sound has no way to travel and cannot be heard, so there is **no sound** in space.

03 **Halley's Comet** is only seen once every 75 to 76 years, and it will not be seen until 2061 when it orbits Earth again.

04 No one actually knows **how many stars** there are in outer space.

05 We know that there are around 200 to 400 billion **stars** in our own galaxy, the Milky Way. There are over a billion galaxies out there with their own stars.

06 **A day** on the planet **Venus** lasts longer than a year on Earth.

07 The Great **Red Spot on Jupiter** is actually a **huge storm** that has been going on for more than 350 years.

08 On the planet Mars, you weigh less. You can **weigh up to 37% less on Mars** than you do on Earth.

09 The **sun** makes up about **99.98%** of **our solar system's total mass**.

10 Planet **Mars** is home to the **tallest volcano** in the solar system. The volcano is three times the size of Mount Everest.

11 Planet **Jupiter** is so large that **Earth** can fit inside of it about **1,000 times**.

12 The **Pistol Star** is the **brightest star** yet discovered. It is ten million times brighter than our sun.

13 Stars are different colors depending on how hot they are. The **hottest stars are blue**, and the **coolest stars are brown**.

14 Somewhere in our galaxy, there is a **black hole** with a mass that is **equal to four billion of our suns**.

15 Every year, the **moon moves away** from Earth by **3.8 centimeters**.

16 "**A cosmic year**" is a name given to the amount of time it takes our sun to revolve fully in the center of the Milky Way, which is about **225 million years**.

17 A **spacesuit** from NASA costs around **$12,000,000** to make. **70%** of that cost goes to making the **control module** and the **backpack**.

18 The planet **Venus** is in fact the **hottest** planet! It has a surface temperature of 450 degrees Celsius even though it is not the closest planet to the sun.

19 The planet **Mercury** is the **closest** planet to the sun, but it is not the hottest because it **has no atmosphere** to regulate the temperature.

20 There is a planet called **55 Cancri E**, which is 40 light-years away, and scientists suspect its surface is made out of **graphite** and **diamonds**.

21 The **footprints left on the moon** will stay there for over **100 million years**.

22 Scientists found **proof of life on Mars** in **1986** in the form of **fossils** of microscopic living things.

23 If **two pieces of metal** are floating around in space and they touch each other then they will be **permanently bonded**. This is called **"cold welding."**

24 The largest discovery of **water** ever found is **in space**. About ten billion light-years away, there is a water vapor cloud carrying a mass of water **140 trillion times** the mass of water in the earth's oceans.

25 **Neutron stars** are the **tiniest** and **densest stars** known to us, and they can spin around 600 times per second.

26 The **moon** was once a **part of the earth that broke off** after the earth was struck by a giant object.

27 Our solar system, the **Milky Way**, is around **4.57 billion years** old.

28 The **sun weighs** approximately **330,000 times** more than the **earth weighs**.

29 There are around **79 moons**, which we know of, **orbiting Jupiter**.

30 **Mars orbits the sun slower** than Earth does. This means that even though a day on Mars is longer than a day on Earth, a year on Mars lasts 687 days, making it **longer than a year on Earth**.

31 If a **star** gets too close to a **black hole** it will be **torn apart**.

32 The planets **Venus** and **Mercury** are the only two planets in the Milky Way that **do not have moons**.

33 A **day on Mars** is a **little longer** than a day on **Earth**. A day on Mars lasts 24 hours, 39 minutes, and 35 seconds.

34 NASA found evidence of **water** on the **moon**.

35 It takes **25 to 35 days** on Earth for the **sun to make a full rotation**.

36 The only reason our oceans have **tides** is because of the **gravitational** pull from the **sun** and the **moon**.

37 **Pluto** is so small that the United States is bigger than it is.

38 **Earth** is the only planet in our solar system that is **not named** after some kind of **god**.

39 No one knows who named our planet "**Earth**."

40 **Venus** has more **volcanoes** on its surface than any other planet in the solar system.

41 There are four planets in our solar system that are called "**Gas Giants**." These planets are known as **Jupiter**, **Saturn**, **Neptune**, and **Uranus**. This is because they are mostly made up of gasses and only have a small rocky core.

42 **Triton**, the moon on Neptune, **orbits** the planet the **opposite way**. It is the only large moon that does this.

43 **Triton** is slowly **moving closer to Neptune**, and soon it will be torn apart by the planet's gravity and become another ring around Neptune.

44 If **Triton** becomes a ring around Neptune, then **Neptune** will have **more rings than Saturn**.

45 There are **ten times more stars** out in space than there are grains of **sand** in the whole of Earth.

46 **27%** of the universe is made up of **dark matter**, and 68% of it is dark energy. These are completely invisible, even with a telescope.

47 Any **liquid in space** floating freely will form itself into a perfect **sphere**.

48 The **largest moon orbiting Pluto**, known as **"Charon,"** is about half of the size of Pluto.

49 A single **season** on **Uranus** will last up to **21 years** on Earth.

50 **Saturn** is the **second-largest** planet in the solar system. It is also the **lightest**. If it were placed in water, it is the only planet that would **float**.

51 Only **5%** of our **universe** is **visible**.

52 **Light from the sun** can travel to the **earth** in **eight minutes** and **20 seconds**.

53 **Outer space** is about **62 miles away** from you if you are standing on the surface of Earth.

54 The word **"astronaut"** is derived from the Greek words **"astron"** and **"nautes,"** which mean **"star"** and **"sailor."** The word "astronaut" means "star sailor."

55 Scientists know more about the **moon** and **Mars** than they do about **Earth's oceans**.

56 It takes the **International Space Station** around 92 minutes to completely **circle the earth**.

57 The **moon**, unlike Earth, **does not rotate** on an axis. This means that the same side of the moon is always facing Earth.

58 On the surface of **Venus**, the **snow is metal** and the **rain is sulfuric acid**.

59 The **first soft drink** to ever be **drunk in space** by astronauts was **Coca-Cola**.

60 Coca-Cola beat Pepsi by only a few minutes; **Pepsi** was the **second soft drink** to be **drunk in space**.

61 Astronauts say that **space smells** like **raspberries, seared steak**, and **rum**.

62 You **cannot burp** in **space**.

63 **Pluto** was named after the **Roman god** of the **underworld**, and the **dog in Disney** was named after the former planet.

64 A **sunset** on the planet **Mars** is actually **blue**.

65 In **China**, they call the **Milky Way** the "**Silver River**."

66 **Pens do not work in space** because there is **no gravity**.

67 It takes the **light from the moon** about **1.3 seconds** to travel to Earth.

68 A **single day on Mercury** lasts up to **58 days** on Earth.

69 The **Giant Red Spot**, which is a huge storm raging on Jupiter, is **shrinking** over time, but it is also getting **taller**.

70 **Laika**, a stray dog from Russia, was the **first living mammal** to be **sent into space**.

71 The **earth weighs 81 times** more than the **moon**.

72 An astronaut named **Gennady Padalka** has the **most time in space** out of anyone else on Earth. He has spent **879 days** in space.

73 **Uranus** was the second name chosen for the planet. It was **originally known** as "**George's Star**."

74 An **astronaut's space helmet** has a **Velcro patch** inside it just in case the astronaut gets an **itch** on their **nose**. This is the only thing it is used for.

75 An "**exoplanet**" is the name given to a **planet that orbits around a star**, much like all of the planets in our solar system.

76 **Valentina Tereshkova** was a Russian woman, and she was the **first woman** to be **launched into space**.

77 The **first spacecraft** to visit **Mercury** was **Mariner 10** in the year **1974**.

78 **Pluto** used to be considered a planet much like Earth and Mars. However, in **2006**, it was classified as a **Dwarf Planet**.

79 The **first black hole** that was ever photographed is around three million times the size of Earth.

80 Around three to seven **galaxies** are **visible** with the naked eye from Earth.

81 Earth, Mars, Venus, and Mercury are all known as **inner planets** because they orbit the closest to the sun.

82 **Pluto** has a slower **rotation** than Earth, so a day on Pluto is the same as 6 days, 9 hours, and 36 minutes on Earth.

83 **Dwarf Planets**, unlike normal planets, are unable to gravitationally dominate the things surrounding their orbit.

84 There are **five Dwarf Planets** in our solar system: Ceres, Eris, Makemake, Haumea, and Pluto.

85 The **Chinese** first began to **document Halley's Comet** in 240 B.C.

86 **Umbrellas** and **gas masks** were once sold as **protection against comets**.

87 **Dwarf Planets** are in their own league because they **cannot be considered asteroids or moons**. They are too big to be asteroids, and their gravitational pull and orbit are different from that of a moon.

88 There was once an **"anti-comet" pill** that was sold. It was believed it gave people **protection against comets falling** on them.

89 There are over 3,000 **comets** we know of in our solar system.

90 There are about 88 **star constellations** you can see in the night sky.

91 **Jupiter** is known as the **solar system's dumping ground** because most asteroids are pulled in by its gravity

92 **Jupiter's strong gravitational** pull has **saved Earth** from many harmful **asteroids** by sucking them in before they can collide with Earth.

93 **Mercury** only **rotates three times** for every two orbits it makes around the sun.

94 Up until **1965**, it was believed that **Mercury** did not rotate at all and the same side of the planet was always facing the sun.

95 **NASA** means the National Aeronautics and Space Administration.

96 **Neptune** needs **165 years** to orbit the sun one time.

97 **Neptune** was discovered in **1846**, and since then, it has only made one orbit around the sun.

98 The **Whirlpool Galaxy**, also known as M51, was the first object in space to be identified as a **spiral**.

99 The **rings of Saturn** are **so thin** that if they were only three feet long, they would be 10,000 times thinner than a razor blade is.

100 **Buzz Lightyear**, a toy from the *Toy Story* movies, has actually been **sent to outer space**. He spent about 15 months in space.

01 It takes 120 **raindrops** to fill one **teaspoon**.

02 A **woman** will spend around **76 days** of her life just rummaging through her **handbag**.

03 The record for the longest **cherry pit spit** was approximately 71.2 feet.

04 **America** has more **plastic flamingos** than real ones.

05 Reginald Dwight is **Elton John's real name**.

06 A collection of **bananas** is usually referred to as a "hand."

07 The **sound of E.T**, from the movie *E.T. the Extra-Terrestrial*, when he was walking, was made using **jelly**.

08 A **python** is so big that it can **swallow a pig whole**!

09 We do not actually know what **color** the **T-Rex** was.

10 An average **human body** contains enough **iron** in the bloodstream to make a nail three inches tall.

11 It cost more to make the **film *Titanic*** than it cost to make the actual Titanic ship.

12 There is a book whose title is 679 words long. It is the **longest title** in the world for a **book**.

13 A **salad** from **McDonald's** is actually more fattening than a burger.

14 There are so many pieces of **Lego** in the world that you could give everyone at least 62 pieces each.

15 **Pearls** may be small, but they can actually weigh up to **13 pounds**.

16 Scientists suggest that the average human will **swallow** about a liter of **snot** every day.

17 It is known that your **eyesight** actually **improves** when you are **scared**.

18 The **fear of heights** and the **fear of clowns** are the two most common fears on Earth.

19 There is enough **carbon in your body** to make around 9,000 pencils.

20 When you go up an **elevator**, you weigh the same, but when you are going down you weigh less.

21 **Rabbits** like to eat **licorice**.

22 On average, you will unknowingly **eat** around 430 **bugs** a year.

23 In the United States, there is currently a **plan** on how the country can deal with a **zombie apocalypse**.

24 **Spiders** are not insects; they are **arachnids**.

25 **Insects** have six **legs**.

26 **Lemon** contains more **sugar** than a strawberry does.

27 The **Aztec Indians** were the ones who invented **popcorn**.

28 **Lobsters** have clear, colorless **blood**, but when their blood is exposed to oxygen, it turns blue.

29 A **bird** needs gravity in order to **swallow**, so birds cannot swallow in space.

30 **Potato chips** are the **most popular snack food** in the entire world.

31 **Reindeer hair** is **like a tube** because it is hollow inside.

32 A **croissant** sounds like it is French, but it was actually invented in **Austria**.

33 There is a type of **beer in Africa** that is brewed from **bananas**.

34 A group of **frogs** is referred to as an **"army."**

35 A large group of **kangaroos** is referred to as a **"mob."**

36 A collection of **geese** is referred to as a **"gaggle."**

37 The **King of Hearts**, in a deck of cards, is the only king of the four that does **not have a mustache**.

38 **Women** purchase **96%** of the **candles** that are sold.

39 Unlike us and some other animals, a **cat** is unable to move its **jaw** to the side.

40 **Domesticated cats** hate the smell of **citrus**.

41 It is forbidden to **hug trees** in **China**.

42 *Mary Poppins*, the film made by Disney, was **filmed** completely **indoors**.

43 **Paper** was originally created in **China**. So was the **wheelbarrow**.

44 You can **spin** a **hardboiled egg**, but a soft boiled or uncooked egg will not spin.

45 A **pearl** will **melt** in vinegar.

46 The name for the **dot** on top of the letter "**I**" is a "**tittle**."

47 About **72%** of **people** in the world will **eavesdrop** on someone.

48 An **ostrich** actually does **not bury its head** in the sand when it is frightened.

49 It is only the **female mosquitoes** that **bite**; the males do not.

50 A **hummingbird cannot walk** at all.

51 The same **company** that builds the **Porsche** also builds **tractors**.

52 **Iguanas** are able to **hold their breath underwater** for up to 28 minutes.

53 **Green diamonds** are the **rarest** diamonds in the world.

54 The average **cow** will produce about **40 glasses** full of **milk a day**.

55 **Men** are seven times more likely to be **struck by lightning** than women are.

56 **Flies** are able to **launch** themselves into the air **backward** so they can make a quick getaway.

57 A **jellyfish** is made up of **95% water**.

58 The **moon** is nine times **brighter** when it is **full** than when it is a half-moon.

59 **Porcupines** have an average of **30,000 spikes**.

60 **Camels** are usually **born without** their **humps**.

61 The people in **Iceland** drink the most **Coca-Cola** out of any other country in the world.

62 **Bees kill** people more than **snakes** do.

63 A **giraffe** does not have any vocal cords, so it technically does **not have a voice**.

64 The **longest word** that you can **type using only your right hand** on a keyboard is "**lollipop**."

65 The only way you are able to **see** a **rainbow** is if your back is facing the sun.

66 The **people** who **work at night** are more likely to **weigh more** than those who work during the day.

67 We use up to **72 different muscles** when we **speak**.

68 The **Mona Lisa** took Leonardo Da Vinci precisely **ten years to paint**.

69 **Giraffes** tend to have the **highest blood pressure** out of any other animal.

70 You can tell the **difference** between **a female and a male horse** by looking at their **teeth**. A female has 36 teeth while a male has 40.

71 There are over **50 million monkeys** in **India**.

72 A **shark** can **smell** a single drop of **blood in the water** from up to 2.5 miles away.

73 A **bottlenose whale** is capable of **diving** to around 3,000 feet under the water in about two minutes.

74 When two **zebras** are standing together, they will face each other so they can keep an eye out for **predators**.

75 **Elephants** communicate in a **sound wave** that is below the frequency that humans can hear, so we cannot hear them talking to each other.

76 A **snake cannot bite** you if it is in a **river** or a **swamp**; it will drown if it tries.

77 A **flea** is able to **accelerate** up to 50 times faster than a space shuttle can.

78 The **colder** the **room** you sleep in, the higher your chances are for having a **nightmare**.

79 Both sides of your body are not usually the same size. Your **left side** will sometimes be **bigger** than your right side. In other words, your left foot, or your left hand, will be slightly larger than your right one.

80 In the country of **Sweden, high school students** get **paid** around $187 a month just to actually go to school.

81 **Clouds** are **higher in the sky** during the day than they are at night.

82 **NASA** has its own **radio station** that is called the "Third Rock Radio."

83 **Carrots** were first grown in **ancient Greece** to use as **medicine**, not to be eaten.

84 When **Coca-Cola** was **originally released** in 1886, it was advertised as an **"intellectual beverage"** which was supposed to help boost brain power.

85 The color of a **chili pepper** has nothing to do with how hot it is; the size does. Usually the **smaller** the pepper, the **hotter** it is.

86 The **earth** is **hit** by over 500 **meteorites** every year.

87 **Coca-Cola** would **actually** be **green** if they did not add the colorant.

88 The guy who invented the cereal **Corn Flakes** was named **John Kellogg**.

89 The ideal **temperature** that will help you **fall asleep** is between 64 and 86 degrees Fahrenheit.

90 **Honey** will **enter your bloodstream** only 20 minutes after you have eaten it.

91 Each one of your **red blood cells** travels between the lungs and other tissues around 75,000 times before it dies. They only live about four months each.

92 **Enamel** is the **hardest substance** in the human body.

93 **Billboards** have been **banned** in the state of **Vermont** for over 45 years in order to preserve the state's natural beauty.

94 Human blood is about six times **thicker than water** is.

95 Over a third of the world's **pineapples** come from **Hawaii**.

96 Mercury is the only metal that can **become liquid** when at **room temperature**.

97 A "**plenum**" is the **opposite** of a "**vacuum**."

98 The average person will **swallow** around 295 times while eating a meal.

99 There are around six people in the world who will **look exactly** like you. They are known as your "**doppelgänger**."

100 The odds of you being **killed** by a **champagne cork** are higher than the odds of you being killed by a poisonous spider.

01 The **blue whale** is the **loudest animal** alive. It makes a noise that can be heard from over 800 kilometers away.

02 **Cows** and **horses** have to **sleep while standing up**. Can you imagine sleeping while standing?

03 When a **hummingbird** is hovering in the air, it can **beat its wings** around 200 times a second.

04 **Otters sleep** while floating on their backs in the water. They hold each other's hands so they do not float away!

05 **Sharks** are the only fish in the ocean that can **blink** with both their eyes.

06 A **crocodile** cannot stick its tongue out at you. Its **tongue** is actually stuck inside its mouth.

07 If you are hiding from a pig, you have to float above him. **Pigs** actually **cannot look up** at all.

08 An **ostrich's eye** is so big that its brain is smaller than its eye.

09 The eggs a **shark** lays are the **biggest eggs** in the world!

10 The **giant squid's eyes** are the largest in the entire world.

11 If you are looking for a **shrimp's heart**, it is in his **head**!

12 A **tiger's skin** is **striped** just like its fur.

13 A **gorilla** can get **sick**, just like humans can.

14 **Bats** are the only **mammals** on Earth that can **fly**!

15 Speaking of **bats**, they **cannot walk** because their leg bones are too thin.

16 A **tarantula**, which is a big, friendly spider, can **survive** up to two years without eating any food.

17 **Kangaroos** use their **tails** for **balance**; if you lift their tail up off the ground it will not be able to hop.

18 You know **cows** can sleep while standing. Well, they can only have **dreams** if they are **lying down**.

19 For every one **human** in the world, there are about one million **ants**.

20 Also, the **weight** of all the **ants** in the world would match the weight of all the **humans** in the world.

21 A **goldfish** gets its **orange color from light**. If you keep one in a dark room, it will turn into a pale fish!

22 **Alligators** can be really old. They can live for up to **100 years**.

23 An **elephant's tooth** can weigh up to nine pounds. That is quite a heavy tooth!

24 Can you eat while hanging upside down? A **flamingo** cannot **eat** unless its **head** is **upside down**.

25 An **anteater's mouth** is only an inch wide. No wonder it cannot eat anything but ants.

26 **Ants** never get tired and they **never sleep**.

27 Speaking of **ants**, they **do not have** any **lungs**!

28 Horses run fast, but an **ostrich** can **run** faster than a horse.

29 Also, the **male ostrich** can **roar** just like a lion does.

30 In **green areas**, like forests and fields, every acre contains about 50,000 **spiders**!

31 The **blue-eyed lemur** is one of only two primates that are not human to have eyes that are truly blue.

32 A **blue whale** can **weigh** the same as 30 fully grown elephants.

33 A **skunk smells** so bad that you can smell it from up to a mile away!

34 There is one species of **butterfly** that lives in **Africa** that is so **poisonous** it can kill up to six cats!

35 A **snake can see** you even with its **eyes closed** because it can actually see through its eyelids.

36 A **hummingbird** is so good at flying that it can even **fly backward**.

37 A **rhino's horn** is not made of bone. It is made out of **compacted hair**.

38 **Sheep** have **four stomachs**! Each one helps them digest their food, but humans only need one.

39 **Cows** also have **four stomachs**. They need each one to help them digest their food.

40 **Polar bears' fur** might look white, but it is actually **transparent**.

41 Speaking of **polar bears**, their **skin** is completely **black**, but you cannot see it underneath the fur.

42 Most people are **killed by** more **crocodiles** than lions **in Africa**.

43 **Cats' whiskers** are used **to check** if they **can fit into or through something**. If their whiskers are too wide, they know they will not fit!

44 **Bees** do not look like they fly very fast, but a bee can fly up to **15 miles per hour**!

45 A **shark's skeleton** is made out of **cartilage**, not bone like ours.

46 **Elephants** are the **largest mammals on land** in the whole world.

47 A **giraffe** only has **seven bones** in its **neck**! That is the same amount of bones a human has in their neck.

48 **Frogs** do not drink water; they soak it in through the skin!

49 **Dogs** have better **hearing** than humans. Their hearing is four times stronger than ours.

50 An **elephant** needs to **drink** at least 210 liters of water a day.

51 Dolphins are **carnivores**! (That means they eat meat.)

52 Cats are very lazy. They can **sleep** between 13 and 14 hours a day!

53 A **wolf** is the **ancestor** of all the breeds of **domestic dogs** in the world.

54 Wolves are also part of the animal group called **"wild dogs,"** which includes coyotes and dingoes. All dogs came from this group of animals at first.

55 Dolphins breathe through the **blowhole** on the top of their head!

56 A **giraffe's tongue** is a blueish purple color, and it is covered in long bristles.

57 Speaking of giraffes, the **bristles** on a **giraffe's tongue** help it **eat thorny plants**.

58 **Frogs** can **see** in front of them, above them, and on the side of them, all at the same time!

59 **Turtles** can actually **breathe** using their **butts**!

60 **Cheetahs** are so **nervous** that some zoos give them support dogs.

61 **Humpback whales** will let **dolphins** ride on their backs for fun.

62 A **hippopotamus' skin** is 1.5 inches thick.

63 **Flamingos** are bright **pink** because of the color of the food they eat.

64 **Giraffes** are the only animals in the whole world that **cannot yawn**.

65 A **bee** needs to use 22 muscles to **sting**!

66 **Cats cannot taste** anything that is **sweet**.

67 **Spiders' blood** is **transparent**, which means it is clear like water.

68 **Snails** move so **slow** it will take them 115 days to travel only a mile.

69 **Dolphins' brains** are actually bigger than a human's brain.

70 **Dolphins** are also considered to be the **most intelligent animals** on the planet.

71 A **rat** cannot **vomit**!

72 **Elephants** are the only mammals on Earth that cannot **jump**.

73 **Rattlesnakes** are still able to **bite** you for up to an hour after they die; this is because of their reflex actions.

74 A **pigeon's feathers** will weigh more than its bones do!

75 The **great horned owl** is the only animal in existence that will **eat a skunk**.

76 If you put an **electric eel** in **salt water**, it will **short-circuit** itself. They need to live in fresh water.

77 In a **goat's eye**, the **pupil** is a **rectangular** shape.

78 A **crocodile's bite** is the **strongest** bite in the world! It is 12 times stronger than a great white shark's bite.

79 Some animals, such as **frogs** and **fish**, can be **frozen** completely during **winter** and then **unfreeze in spring** and be completely unharmed and healthy.

80 If a **shark** swims upside down, it could slip into a coma!

81 **Giraffes' tongues** are over 18 inches long, and they use their tongues to clean their ears.

82 A **newborn baby kangaroo** is so small that it could fit inside a teaspoon.

83 A **koala bear** is so lazy it needs to **sleep** about **22 hours** a day!

84 When a **penguin falls in love**, they will **search** the whole beach for the **perfect pebble** to give to the penguin that they love.

85 An **earthworm** has so much love because it has up to **nine hearts**.

86 A **tiger** can be trained to use a **litter box** just like a normal cat.

87 A single **beaver** can **cut down** up to **200 trees** in a year with its teeth.

88 **Mosquitoes** are attracted to the color **blue**; they really love it!

89 **Penguins mate for life**! They choose one partner to fall in love with and stay with them for their entire lives.

90 **Penguins** have an organ in their **eyes** that turn salt water into fresh water.

91 **Dolphins** communicate with each other using **whistling**, **clicking**, and other sounds. Each dolphin can actually develop its own unique sound.

92 **Americans** tried to **train bats** to **drop bombs** during World War II.

93 Penguins can also stay **underwater** for up to 27 minutes.

94 The **buzzing noise** that most **insects**, such as bees and mosquitoes, make is caused by the rapid movement of their **wings**.

95 If you place even a tiny amount of **alcohol** on a **scorpion** it will be driven crazy and sting itself.

96 A **female rabbit** is called a "**doe**" and a **male rabbit** is called a "**buck**."

97 A **female elephant** can be **pregnant** for up to two whole years.

98 **Lobsters** and **jellyfish** are considered to be **immortal**. Unless killed by something in their environment, they will never die.

99 **Wild parrots** are able to name their children, and that name sticks for life, just like humans.

100 Monkeys, **koala bears**, and **humans** are the only animals on Earth that have unique, individual **fingerprints**.

01 For about **2,000 years**, it was believed that the **earth** was the **center of the universe** and the sun revolved around the earth, not the other way around.

02 **71%** of the earth's surface is made up of the **ocean**.

03 **Earth** is not a perfect sphere. It is actually closer to the shape of an **egg**.

04 Only **7%** of the ocean is covered with **sea ice**.

05 **Libya** is the **hottest** place on Earth. The highest temperature that was ever recorded there was 136 degrees Fahrenheit in the year 1922.

06 **Earth** is not a perfect sphere because the strength of **gravity** around it is **uneven**.

07 The **Great Barrier Reef** is so **large** it can be seen from the moon.

08 There are only **three countries** in the world that have **not adopted** the **metric system**.

09 Antarctica is the **coldest** place on Earth.

10 **Coral reefs** are the **largest living structures** in the world. They are the only natural home that is also living.

11 In the **summer**, due to the metal expanding in the heat, the **Eiffel Tower** can **grow up** to six inches taller.

12 **Columbus** originally believed that the **earth** was actually shaped like a **pear**.

13 A **blue moon**, in which the moon appears blue and full, only appears once in **2.7 years**.

14 The earth is struck by **lightning** at least 6,000 times per minute!

15 **China** is one of the most **elongated** (meaning greater in length) countries in the world.

16 There is a small township in India called **Auroville**. In this town, they have **no money** or **religion**, and they live entirely in peace.

17 The **biggest island** in the world is **Greenland**.

18 There are around **45,000 thunderstorms** occurring around the world **every day**.

19 For some reason, the average **Canadian earns more** than the average **American** and is therefore richer.

20 There are around 1,500 **earthquakes** in **Japan** happening every year.

21 **Lightning** strikes the earth **100 times a second**!

22 **Diamonds** actually are not as rare as you may think. They are very easy to find on Earth.

23 It is not illegal to **escape from prison** in **Denmark**.

24 The **Kawah Ijen volcano** in Indonesia has **luminous blue lava** and a massive **acid lake**.

25 On average, the **ocean** is about **2.7 miles deep**.

26 Only about **10%** of the earth's **population** lives in the **southern hemisphere**.

27 **Hurricanes** that appear over the **ocean** can last up to ten days.

28 Around 8.5 million tons of **water evaporates** from the **Dead Sea** every day.

29 **85%** of all Earth's **plant life** is found in the **ocean**.

30 When **lightning** strikes the earth, it can reach **temperatures** of over 54,000 degrees Fahrenheit. That is hotter than the surface of the sun.

31 The only continent on Earth that does **not have an active volcano** is the **continent Australia**.

32 The water in the **Atlantic Ocean** is **saltier** than the water in the Pacific Ocean.

33 **Hawaii** and **New York** are the two states **surrounded** by the **most ocean water**.

34 Spanish, Mandarin Chinese, and English are the three most common languages spoken in the whole world.

35 Perth is the windiest city in Australia.

36 People in Switzerland eat the most chocolate: 22 pounds per person a year.

37 Yonge Street in Toronto, Canada, is the longest street in the whole world. It is 1,178 miles long.

38 The original name for Australia was "New Holland."

39 The Grand Canyon is so large it can hold up to 900 trillion footballs.

40 The smallest ocean in the world is the Arctic Ocean.

41 Half of the world's oxygen supply is produced by the Amazon rainforest.

42 The country Brazil was named after a tree.

43 The country **Brazil** makes up **50%** of the **South American** continent.

44 There are around **120** different **rivers** in **Jamaica**.

45 The **Great Wall of China** is around **3,995 miles** long.

46 Approximately **50%** of the **world's population** uses **rice** as a staple food.

47 **India** has over 200 million **cows** and 100,000 **post offices**, the most in the world for both.

48 There are more **redheads** in **Scotland** than in any other country in the world.

49 The world's largest collection of **flora** can be found in **Bali**.

50 The original name for **Hawaii** was the "**Sandwich Islands**."

51 The country of **Germany** is the **border** for **nine other countries**.

52 There are more **pyramids** in **Peru** than there are in Egypt.

53 **Tokyo** was once called "**Edo**."

54 The world's **oceans** contain 200 times more **gold** than has already been mined.

55 Around **75%** of the world's **countries** are **north** of the equator.

56 The original name for **New York** was "**New Amsterdam**."

57 The **Dead Sea** is not part of the sea. It is actually a **lake** located inland.

58 **Saudi Arabia** has absolutely **no rivers**.

59 The water in the **Dead Sea** is so **salty** that it is easy to **float** on the water and almost impossible to sink.

60 Up to **32% of land** in the **United States** is owned by the **U.S. government**.

61 Cuba is the largest **exporter** of **sugar** in the world.

62 **Hawaii** only became part of the **United States** in the 1900s.

63 There are 571 miles of **shoreline** in **New York**.

64 **Rio de Janeiro** can be translated into the **"River of January."**

65 **New Zealand's South Island** is the **oldest exposed surface** on Earth.

66 The typical height of a **tsunami wave** in the **Pacific Ocean** is between 19.7 feet to 29.5 feet high.

67 The **Earth weighs** 6,588,000,000,000,000,000 tons. What a mouthful!

68 Up to 80% of the world's **food crops** are **pollinated by insects**.

69 The **ocean** makes up 97% of the whole world's **water** supply.

70 The world's oceans look like they are flat but they are not. Because of the gravity combined with high winds, there are **different levels** of the **sea** around the world.

71 **Earth's temperature** cooled around 3.8 billion years ago, which caused a large amount of water to condense from a gas into water. This is what filled the large basins of water we know today.

72 It takes 1,000 years for the water in the oceans to complete a journey around the world. This is a continuous journey that the ocean's water takes called the "**global ocean conveyor belt**."

73 Half of the **oxygen** that we breathe in is produced by the world's **oceans**.

74 There are about 230,000 **marine species** known to exist in the oceans, and we estimate that there are more than two million species we have not discovered yet.

75 Many of the species that live at the bottom of the ocean, known as "**abyssal creatures**," are able to **glow in the dark**. This is due to a special chemical reaction they trigger in their bodies.

76 A few of the **species** that live in the **Antarctic Ocean** have natural **antifreeze** in their blood, which stops them from freezing in the cold water.

77 Only 1% of the **ocean floor** is covered by **coral reefs**. About 25% of all marine life in the oceans calls the coral reef their home.

78 **Coral reefs** take **years** to **grow** even by an inch, so it is very important that they do not get damaged.

79 Only 5% of the **ocean floor** has been mapped in detail. The remaining **95%** is still **undiscovered**.

80 The **Mariana Trench** is thought to be the **deepest trench** in the world's oceans.

81 The **deepest living fish** discovered in the oceans is known as the "**ghost fish**," and it lives 26,715 feet deep.

82 Earth used to be dry and barren with no oceans at all. All of the water was tapped within the earth, and when the **earth's temperature changed drastically** all those years ago, the water was released.

83 The largest known **blue whale** to live is known to be the same height as an 11-story building.

84 About 97% of the world's **habitable space** is in the **oceans**.

85 **Sicily** is the **largest island** in the **Mediterranean Sea**.

86 **Canada** has more **lakes** than any other country in the entire world.

87 Up to 90% of the world's **volcanic activity** occurs in the **ocean**.

88 The **Nile River** in Egypt is known to always **flow north**.

89 The earth will experience over 50,000 **earthquakes**, on average, in an entire year.

90 The average **iceberg** will **weigh** around 20,000,000 tons.

91 About 98% of **Antarctica** is **ice** while the other 2% is **barren rock**.

92 The country of **Finland** has the **most islands** in the whole world, which is just over 179,550 islands.

93 **Vatican City** is the **smallest country** in the world; it only takes up 0.2 square miles.

94 Every single **living thing** on Earth contains a certain amount of **carbon**.

95 A **mature oak tree** will **shed** around 700,000 leaves during **autumn**.

96 Of all of the water on Earth, 97% is **salt water** and 3% is **fresh water**. Of that 3%, 2% of it is contained in ice sheets and glaciers in the ocean.

97 The continent of **Asia** covers around 30% of the **land** on Earth but holds 60% of the world's **population**.

98 **Earth's atmosphere** is around 60 miles **thick**.

99 The **Dead Sea** is the **lowest point** that can be found on land. It is 1,388 feet below sea level.

100 Around 300 million years ago, Earth had only one massive continent known today as **"Pangaea."** Later on, the continents split and drifted apart to form the earth we have today.

101 Scientists suggest that **life on Earth** used to be purple rather than green.

102 The **continents** are **still shifting**. A few million years into the future, the continents will most likely drift back into one massive continent.

103 Every day **dust from space falls** to Earth, and its particles are so small that we cannot see them.

104 **Coastlines in America** make up about 20% of the land area, but around 50% of the population in the United States lives on just that 20% of the land.

105 The **General Sherman giant sequoia** is a tree, and it is the biggest living thing on Earth.

106 We know that the **first life on Earth** started in the oceans and eventually evolved and moved onto land.

107 **Manila**, a city in the Philippines, is the **most crowded** city in the world with 1,660,714 people living in just 14.8 square miles of space.

108 On the other hand, **Greenland** is the **least crowded** area on Earth. It stretches to over 836,330 square miles of space, and only 56,534 people live there.

109 The **Atacama Desert** is the **driest** spot on Earth. There are places in the middle of this desert that have never seen rain.

110 Our **atmosphere** is made up of 78% **nitrogen** and 21% **Oxygen**. The other 1% is made up of trace amounts of **different gasses** including carbon dioxide.

111 The **lowest point** in the earth is in the ocean, and it is called **"Challenger Deep."** It reaches further down than Mount Everest reaches up.

112 **Earth's orbit** around the sun is the **most circular** orbit out of all the planets.

113 Around 90% of an **iceberg** is **underneath** the **water's surface**. What you see on top is only 10% of its total size.

114 The **Great Barrier Reef** is the world's **largest living structure**.

115 **Earth formed** at the same time as the rest of the solar system, so all of the planets are around the same age as Earth.

116 **Earth** is the third rock from the sun and it is the fifth-largest rock in the solar system.

117 The **ocean** is one of the **most used** means of **transport** across the globe, mostly by shipping companies and not actual people.

118 The **Pacific Ocean's name** can be translated into "**peaceful sea**."

119 There are about 25,000 different **islands** in the **Pacific Ocean** alone. This is actually more than it is found in the rest of the earth's oceans.

120 The **Atlantic Ocean** is the second-largest ocean on Earth, taking up 21% of the Earth's surface. The Pacific Ocean takes up 30%.

121 The **Arctic Ocean** is completely covered in sea ice during the winter.

122 The **Pacific Ocean** is surrounded by something called the **"Pacific Ring of Fire,"** which is a large collection of active volcanoes.

123 The third-largest ocean is the **Indian Ocean**, and it only takes up about 14% of the earth's surface.

124 The **Bermuda Triangle**, one of the biggest **mysteries** on Earth, is located in the **Atlantic Ocean**.

125 The **Southern Ocean** is the area of water that surrounds **Antarctica**, but some argue whether or not it counts as an ocean itself or if it is just part of another ocean.

126 You will find **turtles** living on every single continent in the world **except Antarctica**.

127 **Earth's rotation** has been slowing down since the beginning. It is suspected that because of this, a day on Earth during the time of the dinosaurs would have been only 22 hours long.

128 Humans, and **most other things on Earth**, are made up of the **same material** that **stars** are made out of.

129 You will find **spiders** everywhere on Earth **except in Antarctica**.

130 It is suspected that up to 2,000 **new species** are **discovered** either in our oceans or on the land every year.

131 **Sunlight** cannot penetrate the **ocean** deeper than 665 feet, so everything else below that is in permanent darkness.

132 When a **tsunami** is **forming out** in the ocean nearby, the only way to tell is by going to the beach. The water on a **beach** nearby a forming tsunami will **recede** as the tsunami is pulling all of the water towards itself.

133 The **Sargasso Sea** is the only sea that does **not have** a **coastline**.

134 The **Sargasso Sea** is linked to the mysterious happenings of the **Bermuda Triangle**, and it is said that it steals people from their boats. Many boats have been found floating around in that sea without anyone on board.

135 There is a **single glacier** that contributes to 10% of all of the **meltwater** in the world, which is causing the sea level to rise slightly over the years.

136 **Earth's core** is as hot as the sun's surface.

137 The **Yew Tree** is the **most toxic plant** on Earth.

138 Only 0.0003% of the **water** on Earth can **safely** be used by humans.

139 **Earth** is **electric** and slightly **radioactive**.

140 **Hudson Bay**, in Canada, has the **lowest gravity** of any part of the earth.

141 There are about three times the **number of atoms** in a **teaspoon** of water than there are teaspoons of water in the **Atlantic Ocean**.

142 **Mawsynram**, located east of Meghalaya, is dubbed the **wettest place** on Earth. It gets around 467.4 inches of rainfall every year.

143 **Hang Son Doong**, located in Vietnam, is the **largest cave** in the world. It is over approximately 656 feet high, and it is so large, it has its own climate with rivers, jungles, and even clouds.

144 In **Russia**, there is a lake called "**Lake Baikal**." It is the oldest lake in the world and it is also the deepest lake. It is famous for holding one-fifth of all the fresh water in the world.

145 There is a spot in the United States called the "**Four Corners**," and in this spot, you can **stand in four different states** at once. It is the spot where Utah, New Mexico, Arizona, and Colorado meet.

146 **Dolphins** in the ocean are **typically blue**, but the dolphins in the **Amazon River** are usually **pink**.

147 If the amount of **oxygen** in the atmosphere **doubled**, we would be happier, paper airplanes would fly further before coming to the ground, we would be more physically active and alert, but there would also be giant insects.

148 There is a type of **mushroom** that grows on Earth that if you eat it once, you will feel fed for the rest of your life.

149 There is a spot on Earth called **"The Door to Hell."** It is a hole filled with **natural gas**. In the year 1971, scientists set fire to the natural gasses expecting them to only burn for a few minutes; however, they have been burning nonstop since then.

150 The **lightest material** in the world is called a **"graphene aerogel."** It is made up of 99.8% air, but it can hold 4,000 times more than its own weight.

151 The distance from New York to Los Angeles is greater than the **diameter** of the **moon**!

152 Eight out of ten of the **most expensive disasters** in the history of the United States have been due to **hurricanes**.

153 An Australian man attempted to **sell New Zealand** on eBay in 2006.

154 A type of **rainbow** can be created from the **light of the moon**, and it is called a **moonbow**.

155 A place on Earth called **"Ethiopia"** has a **13-month** long year, and they are still living in the year 2009.

156 There is a village in Wales that is named "Llanfairpwllgwyngyllgogerychwyrndrobwllllantysiliogogogoch." It is the **longest name** of a **place** in the whole world.

157 There was a **massive earthquake** in **Japan** in 2011. This earthquake **shortened the days** on Earth by about 1.8 microseconds.

158 If the whole **earth** was **compressed** into the size of a marble, it would eventually collapse on itself and form a black hole.

159 If the **world lost oxygen** for only **five seconds**, everyone at the beach would get sunburnt instantly, the daytime sky would darken like nighttime, the earth's crust would begin to crumble, concrete buildings would turn to dust, and the oceans would instantly evaporate into a gas.

160 There is a **tree** in the United States that **cannot be cut down** because it legally owns itself along with about eight feet of land around it.

161 Around ten million years ago, after the extinction of dinosaurs, there were **turtles so large** roaming the earth that they could eat a crocodile in a single bite.

162 Scientists believe that the reason for **Earth** having a **magnetic field** is due to the fact that it has a liquid metal core; however, this is not yet proven.

163 Different members of the same species that live in the ocean can **grow** to **different sizes** depending on **how deep** in the **ocean** they live. Those that live deeper in the ocean tend to grow larger than those that live closer to the surface. No one knows why this happens, but it is a common occurrence in animals that live in the deepest parts of the ocean.

164 The **Opah** is the only **warm-blooded fish** species in the whole world.

165 Approximately 33 feet below the surface of the ocean, **color** is said to be affected by the **scarcity of light**. Blood appears green because you cannot see yellow or red at this depth in the ocean.

166 **Scuba diving** in the ocean is safer than skydiving, driving, and even running a marathon.

167 One inch of the **ocean's depth** contains as much **water** as **Earth's atmosphere**.

168 There is 50 times **more carbon** in the **ocean** than there is in the earth's atmosphere.

169 Only eight feet of the **ocean's depth** can hold as much **heat** as the earth's atmosphere.

170 Some species of **deep-sea coral** live as deep as 19,685 feet, and the water down there is as cold as 35 degrees Fahrenheit.

171 The largest **underwater cliffs** can be found in the **Bahamas**. The cliffs are 4,000 meters high.

172 If all the **mid-ocean ridges** were combined, they could stretch around the earth twice.

173 The world's **longest mountain chain** exists underneath the ocean. It is called the "**Mid Oceanic Ridge**," and it is approximately 40,389 miles long.

174 Even though **Antarctica** holds 90% of the world's ice and around 70% of its fresh water, it is actually considered to be a **desert**. It only gets around two inches of rain a year in the form of snow.

175 702 feet is the **deepest free dive** into the ocean that anyone has ever done.

176 1,090 feet and 4.5 inches are the **deepest** anyone has ever **scuba dived** into the ocean.

177 The **deepest dive** into the ocean mankind has ever done, using a **manned vessel**, was 36,089 feet.

178 Although it does not feel as though you are moving when you are standing still, you are. The **earth** is **spinning** through space at around 1,000 miles per hour.

179 The **largest earthquake** ever recorded was in **Alaska** in 2016.

180 It is believed that Earth once had **two moons**; however, we suspect that the second, smaller moon had crashed into our current moon. It was destroyed and it changed one side of the current moon so that it is drastically different from the other side.

181 Some people believe that you can see **The Great Wall of China** from space, but you actually cannot.

182 At the pancake-flat lakebed known as **"Racetrack Playa"** in Death Valley, **rocks can walk**. For some reason, in this particular part of the world, a slight breeze can pick up a rock and make it walk across the lake bed. A storm has been known to pick up rocks that weigh tens and hundreds of pounds.

183 **Reinhold Messner** and **Peter Haveler** were the first two people to climb to the top of **Mount Everest without** the help of **oxygen** tanks.

184 Due to **climate change**, we are losing our supply of fresh water because the **icebergs** and **glaciers** are **melting** into the sea.

185 The reason we have **daytime** and **night time** is that the earth is spinning on an axis at the same time it is spinning around the sun. When it is night time by you, it is actually daytime on the other side of the world.

186 **Earth** is in what is called the **"Goldilocks Zone"** in our solar system. It is the perfect distance away from the sun so that it is not too hot or too cold. It also has oxygen and water. These are the only things a planet needs to sustain life, and Earth is the only planet in our solar system that has all of it!

187 The sun does not warm space because space does not have an atmosphere. Our **atmosphere** is responsible for turning the **sun's rays** into **heat** for us.

188 **Earth** is the only planet in the solar system that has **plate tectonics**, which is responsible for several things that make life possible on Earth. Without the tectonic plates, our planet would overheat, like Venus.

189 The **size comparison** between the **sun** and the **earth** can be explained by imagining the front door of your house and a nickel sitting in front of it. The sun is the front door and the earth is the nickel.

190 The **Sahara Desert** is one of the largest, **most barren** places on Earth, and yet it helps the Amazon rainforest survive. Every year, the Sahara Desert supplies the Amazon rainforest with 40 million tons of dust that is transported there by wind over the oceans. Without this dust, the Amazon rainforest would not be able to grow and provide us with oxygen the way it does.

191 A **supervolcano's explosion** could be powerful enough to **change** the **shape** and **course** of the world. It could plunge the world into a new ice age if one were to erupt and flood the world with ash.

192 At the last count, there were around 1,500 **active volcanoes** on Earth above the ocean, but it is only the ones known as "supervolcanoes" that you have to worry about.

193 The **world today** is so different from how it was when dinosaurs were still alive that dinosaurs would not be able to survive on Earth now, and we would not be able to live at the same time as they did. This is mostly due to the difference in **oxygen levels.**

194 The **earth's atmosphere** is built to **protect** us from the 100 tons of **meteorites** that enter our atmosphere every day. The meteorites are broken up and turned to dust in the air before they have a chance to hit the ground and cause some damage.

195 **China's air pollution** is so bad that it can be seen from space. The air around China appears as a brownish-grey color due to its high level of pollution.

196 There is an **island between Canada and Denmark** that is still disputed territory between the two countries. Military members from each country often go to the island to remove the other country's flag and replace it with their own.

197 **Earthquakes** actually move the earth underneath the ocean, and that is what causes large waves that turn into **tsunamis**.

198 The **North Pole switches sides** with the **South Pole** every 200,000 to 300,000 years, and this is referred to as the magnetic flip-flop.

199 3,000 people have visited the top of **Mount Everest**, which is the highest point in the world, but only three people have visited the **Challenger Deep**, which is the deepest part of the world.

200 There is a **hidden continent** on Earth called "**Zealandia**." This continent broke off of Australia and sank to the bottom of the ocean about 65 to 80 million years ago.

FACTS *to* HELP TIME TRAVELERS

01 There was a war that only lasted for 38 minutes, and it is the **shortest war** in history.

02 10,000 years was the **longest jail sentence** ever passed.

03 The **bacteria** in your **ear** are increased by 700 times if you wear **headphones** for an hour.

04 "Planck time" is the name given to the **smallest scientific measure of time**.

05 The creation of **instant coffee** was only in 1901.

06 Our **universe** is around 13.8 billion years old.

07 The **International Fixed Calendar** has **13 months** instead of 12.

08 A **year** contains a total of 31,557,600 **seconds**.

09 In 63 years, humans progressed from taking our **first airplane flight** to **landing on the moon**.

10 There is a clock called the "**Strontium Atomic Clock,**" and it is the **most accurate** teller of time ever built.

11 There is a clock that uses the position of the sun to measure time by casting a shadow. It is called a "**sundial.**"

12 **Julius Caesar** invented the **leap year** in 46 B.C.

13 The first **modern clock** was invented in 1511 by a man named **Peter Henle**.

14 1,000,000,000,000 years is called a "**gigayear.**"

15 The **longest eclipse** of the **sun** that is possible is about 7.31 minutes long.

16 The time zone that the **International Space Station** follows is **GMT**.

17 An average human will **blink** around 25,000 times a day.

18 It takes the **moon** 27.32 days to **fully orbit** the earth.

19 **Julius Caesar** created the **Julian calendar**, which was based around the earth's rotations around the sun.

20 **Russia**, the **largest country** of the world, has to use up to **11 consecutive time zones**.

21 During the **Mesozoic Era**, when dinosaurs were still roaming the earth, a year contained about 370 days.

22 **Alaska** and **Hawaii**, although really far away from one another, have the **same time zone**.

23 The study of devices that are used to measure time and the scientific study of **time** itself is called "**Horology**."

24 **Greenland** is known as the world's **largest island**, and it has to use **four** different **time zones**.

25 The Sunday that comes directly after the first full moon after the Spring Equinox is known as "**Easter**."

26 **Daylight Saving** is when we have to turn all the clocks forward by an hour in order to keep the **correct time**.

27 The idea of **Daylight Saving** was first proposed by **Benjamin Franklin**, although his proposal was a similar solution but not actually Daylight Saving.

28 The **longest time** spent playing a **board game** is 80 hours!

29 The continent of **Australia** needs to have both a vertical and a horizontal **time zone** during the **summer**.

30 **China** has been divided into **five time zones** because it is so big.

31 A study showed that most **serial killers** are more likely to be **born in November**.

32 **Kissing** someone for an entire minute burns around 26 **calories**.

33 It takes around 550 thousand trillion, trillion, trillion Planck seconds to **blink** once.

34 During the **last ice age**, beavers were as large as bears.

35 We all know that **February** has 28 days, except during a leap year when it has 29 days. Did you know that February 30th has been an actual day in history?

36 **Einstein** once said that there was no distinction between the past, present, and future because they are all an illusion.

37 **Time** does not actually exist. It is just a concept that we all agree on in order to keep track of the days.

38 3:44 in the morning is the average time people usually **wake up** for no apparent reason at all.

39 Humans first started **eating cooked food** as far back as 1.9 million years ago.

40 Around 400 million years ago, the earth was **covered in** 24-foot **mushrooms** instead of trees.

41 If you are **angry** for a minute, it **weakens your immune system** for up to four or five hours.

42 The **human body sheds** all of its **skin** every four weeks.

43 **Time moves slower** for animals like chipmunks, hummingbirds, and other small rodents.

44 A **day** does **not** last **24 hours**. It takes the earth 23 hours, 56 minutes, and 4.2 seconds to rotate one time.

45 There is a **crystal** that is 4.4 billion years old, and it is considered the **oldest object** on Earth. It is only 160 million years younger than the earth itself.

46 It **takes time for light from objects**, such as the sun and the stars, to reach us. In other words, the light that we see is already in the past.

47 The saying "Time flies when you are having fun" is actually not true. Research shows that **time** actually **slows down** when you are **enjoying** yourself.

48 We know that the **universe began** around 15 billion years ago with the **big bang**, but we have no idea exactly when the **universe will end**.

49 The **sun** has been around for five billion years while **Earth** has been around for about 4.5 billion years.

50 Oxford University has been around longer than the Aztecs.

51 There are **whales** in the ocean with 200-year-old ivory spear tips still lodged in their flesh.

52 The average **human's heart beats** around 100,000 times a day.

53 **China** made up 33% of the world's **GDP** in 1820. Today, it only makes up around 4.5%.

54 The **first calendar** only contained **ten months** and started in March. It was based on the phases of the moon.

55 In 2011, there was a study done that showed four **babies** were being **born** every second of every day.

56 The same study showed that two people **die** every second of every day.

57 By the time the average human turns 70 years old, their **heart** will have **beaten** around 2.5 billion times.

58 The **Roman calendar** did not assign a specific month to winter. This made the whole year 304 days long with 61 of those days making up winter.

59 **Julius Caesar**, a well-known Roman general and statesmen, was the one that introduced the months of **July**, named after him, and **August**, named after his successor.

60 In the year 1836, a man named **John Belville** used to charge people money to tell them what time it was.

61 If a **lightning strike** is seen at least three seconds before thunder is heard, it means that the lightning strike happened about 0.6 miles away.

62 The **Sumerians** were the first civilization in history known to keep **track** of **time** and have a calendar of their own.

63 During the 16th century B.C., people in **Babylon** kept time using **bowls** filled with **water**.

64 According to the **laws of physics**, the faster you move, the slower time moves around you. If you moved faster, you would live longer.

65 A person who **sleeps** an average of eight hours a night will sleep around 229,961 hours during their lifetime.

66 The day of **April** 11th, 1954 is known as the day when nothing happened.

67 We call ten years a "**decade**," 100 years a "**century**," and finally, 1,000 years a "**millennium**."

68 The **moon** was used to create **calendars** around 6,000 years ago.

69 The number of **blinks** the average human has a day is equivalent to having your eyes closed for about 30 minutes.

70 **Niagara Falls** has so much water that it could fill a bathtub every second.

71 The **Taj Mahal** is one of the **oldest buildings** in the world.

72 A **tree** does **not have** a **life expectancy**. If unaffected by nature or man, a tree will continue to grow for eternity.

73 The average human has **hiccups** for around five minutes.

74 A **hummingbird's wings flap** around 90 times a second.

75 It takes less time for dirty **snow** to **melt** than it does for clean snow.

76 The **most common** time for humans to **wake up** is 7 a.m.

77 A person was once in a coma for 37 years, and that is the **longest time** anyone has been in a **coma**.

78 A **housefly** has a **reaction time** of 30 milliseconds, which is why it is difficult to swat one.

79 A **moment** actually lasts around one minute and 30 seconds. This is according to the **old English time system**.

80 If the **events on Earth** from the beginning of time until now were compressed into just 24 hours, the existence of humans would start at 40 seconds before midnight.

81 A container made of **plastic** will take an average of 50,000 years to start **decomposing**.

82 There is a name for a **15th anniversary**. It is called a "**quindecennial**."

83 The **Stonehenge** in England is only around 5,000 years old.

84 The average human can go a few weeks **without food**, but they will die after ten days **without sleep**.

85 During the **1900s** in the **United States**, the average **lifespan** was around 47 years.

86 The average human will produce enough **saliva** to fill two average-sized swimming pools in their lifetime.

87 It would take you about 193 years to **drive to the sun** if you were driving at a constant 55 miles per hour.

88 It takes a **cheetah** only three seconds to go from zero miles per hour to 43 miles per hour.

89 We have found **fossils** of **cockroaches** that are over 280 million years old.

90 **Earth** was **created** on a Saturday evening, on October 22nd, in the year 4004 B.C.

91 The **longest flight** of a **chicken** on an **airplane** was about 13 seconds long.

92 The **first telephone book** was made in 1878, and it only contained 50 names.

93 We only started using **plastic bottles** for **soft drinks** in 1970. Before, we used glass bottles and metal cans.

94 The **Chinese** have been using **fingerprints** to identify one person from another as far back as 700 A.D.

95 As far as we know, most **dinosaurs** would have only lived for a little over a hundred years.

96 **Dinosaurs** were known to have ruled the earth for over 165 million years.

97 **Sharks** are one of the **oldest animals** on Earth. They have been known to have existed here for over 400 million years.

98 If you **spend a year** at the top of **Mount Everest**, it would be 15 microseconds shorter than a year spent at **sea level**.

99 In **Russia, weekends** were **abolished** in 1931 to improve productivity. They went back to a seven-day week only in 1941.

100 A **nanosecond** is the equivalent of one billionth of a second.

FACTS
You
CAN EAT

01 The **most expensive pizza** in the world is known to take around 72 hours to make and is made by three private chefs in your home. It costs $12,000 for just one pizza.

02 **Ranch dressing** is dyed using titanium dioxide, which is also used in sunscreen and paint, in order to make it appear whiter.

03 **Nutmeg** contains a compound called "**myristicin.**" If you eat a large amount of nutmeg, this compound will make you **hallucinate**.

04 The **pound cake** is called that because its original recipe called for a pound of eggs, a pound of butter, and a pound of sugar.

05 Most **fruit-flavored snacks** have a **shine** on them, and this shine is caused by **carnauba wax**, which is also used on cars.

06 Just one **burger** from a fast-food restaurant can contain meat from 100 different cows.

07 **Peanut oil** is used when making **dynamite**!

08 **Ketchup** was used as **medicine** in the early 1800s. It was believed that it could treat indigestion and diarrhea.

09 During this time in the 1800s, there was a special recipe that was used to turn **ketchup** into a **pill**.

10 **Crackers** have **holes** in them because the holes stop air bubbles from forming while the crackers are baking. This prevents the crackers from being ruined.

11 The **burn** you feel from **chili peppers** is fake. A chemical called **"capsaicin"** tricks your mouth into feeling the burn from spicy food.

12 **White chocolate** does not contain any of the components used in actual chocolate, which means that it is not actually chocolate.

13 **Wild salmon** are **pink** because they eat shrimp. Farmed salmon do not eat shrimp so they are white. Before selling them, the farmers dye the salmon pink.

14 The **first ice cream cone** was introduced to the world in 1904.

15 Crackers cause more **damage** to your **teeth** than sugar does.

16 In **Russia**, until 2013, **alcoholic beverages** containing 10% or less alcohol, such as beer, were actually not considered alcoholic. They were considered soft drinks!

17 The **beetle** called "**Dactylopius coccus**" is crushed and boiled in order to produce the **red tint** on most strawberry, cherry, and raspberry flavored candy, such as the red Skittles.

18 **Processed cheese** is also known as American cheese, but it was actually first made in Switzerland.

19 Speaking of **cheese**, it is the **most stolen food** in the world! Around 4% of the world's cheese ends up stolen.

20 **Chocolate** is so good that it was once used as **currency** by different civilizations in South America and Mexico.

21 "**Arachibutyrophobia**" is the name for the **fear of peanut** butter, specifically the fear of getting it stuck to the roof of your mouth.

22 The **expiration date** on **water bottles** is not for the water but for the actual bottle.

23 **Water** can **never expire**, so ignore the "best by" date!

24 **Honey** is actually **bee vomit**!

25 **Nutella** uses up about 25% of the world's **hazelnuts**. One out of every four hazelnuts will end up in a jar of Nutella.

26 Studies have shown that **listening** to **loud music** can make you **drink faster** and drink **more**.

27 The **Froot Loops cereal** might be made of all different colors, but they all actually taste the same.

28 It can take between 144 to 411 **licks** to reach the center of a **tootsie pop**, with the average amount of licks being 364.

29 During **ancient Egyptian** times, **workers** were **paid** with garlic, radishes, and onions, with radishes being the favorite.

30 French fries are not actually French; they were first made in **Belgium**.

31 A **pineapple** technically is not known as a fruit. It is a bunch of berries that have fused together to form one **giant berry**.

32 **Strawberries** cannot be considered berries because usually berries only have seeds on the inside.

33 **Pineapples** have nothing to do with pine or pine trees. When they were first discovered, they were thought to **looked like** a **pine cone**.

34 **Chefs** in **Japan** have to be **trained** for more than two years before they can serve someone a **pufferfish**.

35 If someone eats **pufferfish** that is **not prepared properly**, it can **kill** them.

36 It is thanks to **Thomas Jefferson** that **pasta** is famous in the **United States**. He spent some time in France and brought a macaroni machine back to the United States with him.

37 The **cream** in the center of a **Twinkie** is not actually cream. It is **vegetable shortening**.

38 No one knows where the **first recipe** for **chocolate chip** cookies came from, although there are several theories.

39 **Thomas Jefferson** is also responsible for **introducing Americans** to **mac and cheese**.

40 **Cauliflower** comes in **many different colors**, including purple, green, and orange, though we typically only see the white variety.

41 The **Margherita pizza** is named after Queen Margherita. She loved it so much after eating it during her visit to Naples with her husband King Umberto I.

42 If you place eggs in water, the **rotten eggs** will **float**, and the **fresh** ones will **sink**.

43 The German chocolate cake is not German and has nothing to do with Germany. It was invented by a Texan using German chocolate, which is only called that because of its creator, Sam German.

44 Raw lima beans have enough **cyanide** in them to **kill** you. However, if the lima beans are properly cooked, then they are safe to eat.

45 Not all wine is **vegan**. Some wines contain egg whites, milk protein, gelatin, and sometimes even fish bladder protein.

46 If you want to know if a **cranberry** is **ripe**, drop it to the ground. Ripe cranberries will **bounce** like a ball.

47 According to the **FDA**, there is actually an allowance for **insects** in **food products**.

48 The **popsicle** was invented by accident when an 11-year-old boy left some water and soda in a cup overnight to freeze.

49 In the country of **China, bird saliva** is considered to be known as a delicacy. There is a dish called "**Bird's Nest Soup**."

50 **Food** will **taste different** in an **airplane** than it does on the ground. This is because a higher altitude changes your body's chemistry.

51 Chewing on **coffee beans** can get rid of bad breath.

52 **Orange juice** is one of the main ingredients in **Mountain Dew.**

53 The name "**Chimichanga**," given to a type of food, actually means "**thingamajig.**"

54 **Humans** share 60% of our **DNA** with **bananas**!

55 **Potatoes** are made up of up to 80% **water**.

56 **Turkey** sure does **love tea**. They consume the most tea per person in the world. That is almost seven pounds of tea a year.

57 Before **kale** became popular around 2010, Pizza Hut purchased the most kale out of the whole nation, and they only used it as a garnish at their salad bars.

58 **Pule cheese**, which is made from **donkey milk** in Serbia, is the most expensive cheese in the world. It costs over $1,000 per pound.

59 There is a **difference** between **jam** and **jelly**. Jelly is made with fruit juice while jam is made with fruit.

60 **India** consumes the **least amount** of **meat** in the whole world.

61 Due to the reproductive process of a wasp, **figs** may contain the decomposed body of a **wasp**.

62 The country of **India** is known to be the largest producer and consumer of **chili peppers** in the whole world.

63 Around 49% of all **Americans** over the age of 20 eat at least one **sandwich** every day.

64 Each person in the **Netherlands** drinks about 2.5 cups of **coffee** a day. That is the most in the world.

65 **Nutritious food costs** up to ten times more than **junk food**.

66 **Fortune cookies** were invented in San Francisco in the early 1900s, and they are not Chinese.

67 Tonic water can actually **glow in the dark**!

68 It is so cold in the **Arctic** that people use **refrigerators** to stop their food from freezing.

69 It is **illegal** to **throw food away** in Seattle, Washington.

70 Up to 40% of the **produce** that is grown does **not get sold** simply because it is **too ugly**.

71 **Sound** actually **changes** how **food tastes**. High frequency makes things sweeter, whereas low frequency makes things more bitter.

72 Opposite to India, **Australians eat** the **most meat** out of the whole world.

73 **Americans** eat 500 million pounds of **peanut butter** a year.

74 "**Breakfast is the most important meal of the day**" was a **lie** used by a company called General Foods to sell more cereal.

75 It does not matter how hot it is outside; you **cannot cook** an **egg** on the **sidewalk**.

76 **Cow's milk** can turn pink if the cow eats too many carrots.

77 There is a plant called a "**Pomato**," which can produce both **tomatoes** and **potatoes**.

78 The **pecan nut** is **Alabama's state** nut. They have a pecan festival each year!

79 The **first food grown** in **space** was **red romaine lettuce**, and it was eaten by astronauts in 2015.

80 Enough **Nutella** is sold each year to cover The Great Wall of China eight times.

81 There are about 15,000 **Indian restaurants** in London. That is more than there are in Delhi or Mumbai.

82 The **Margherita pizza** was originally made to match the **colors** of the Italian flag.

83 **Breast milk** is the only food in existence that can provide you with **all the nutrients** your body needs. You could survive off of drinking it alone and nothing else.

84 **California** is in the top five out of all the **food producers** in the whole world.

85 There is a blue banana called the **Blue Java banana** that has a **vanilla taste**.

86 If you do **not eat** food **before going to bed**, your body will burn more fat while you sleep.

87 It would take you 20 years to eat all of the **varieties** of **apples** even if you ate an apple a day.

88 **Cotton candy**, which is famously known for being bad for your teeth, was co-created by a dentist.

89 About 70% of the **spice** in the world comes from **India**.

90 A study was conducted that proved that **hot chocolate** tastes better out of an orange cup.

91 You can find traces of **wood pulp** inside **shredded cheese**.

92 **Goat meat** is the **most popular meat eaten** in the world. Approximately 70% of the world's red meat is goat meat.

93 **Pizza Hut** once delivered a pizza to the **top of Kilimanjaro**, which is the record for the **highest pizza delivery** in the world.

94 You should **keep** your **bananas separate** from the rest of your fruit because bananas make other fruits go bad faster.

95 A year after opening **Domino's pizza**, **James Monaghan**, the co-founder, traded his half of the company for a used VW Beetle.

96 **Spaghetti** is the **plural form** of the word. **Spaghetto** is the **singular form**.

97 The **Galmburger** is the **most expensive burger** in the world, and it costs $1,768.

98 38 years after the opening of **Domino's pizza**, **Tom Monaghan**, the other co-founder, sold his share of the company for $1 billion.

99 **Salt** was worth its weight in **gold** during **Roman** times. Roman soldiers were often paid with salt.

100 **Coriander** and **cilantro** are not the same thing. Cilantro is the plant's leaves and stems, whereas coriander is the dried seeds.

01 The average **temperature** of a **fart**, when it is created, is around 98.6 degrees Fahrenheit.

02 **High heels** were not created for women. They were **originally made for men** who ride horses.

03 When **George Bush**, one of the presidents of the U.S., was in high school, he was a cheerleader.

04 The **first toy** to be **advertised on television** was **Mr. Potato Head**.

05 A study showed that you can **charge** an **iPhone** with **oranges**. It takes 595 oranges to fully charge one.

06 Some people have a **fear** of **going to bed**. This fear is called "**Clinophobia**."

07 Originally, the name for the **boy** that **took care of cows** was a **coward**!

08 The average **human farts** enough gas in a day to fill a **balloon**.

09 When **Walt Disney** won an **Oscar** for the movie *Snow White and the Seven Dwarfs*, they gave him one normal-sized Oscar and seven miniature ones.

10 On average, you **fart** about **14 times a day**.

11 A **New Yorker** is ten times more likely to **bite** you than a shark.

12 The **fear of ducks** watching you is called "**anatidaephobia**."

13 **Reindeer** like to eat **bananas**.

14 A **cow** is able to go up a flight of stairs, but it cannot go back down.

15 A **dragonfly** has six legs, but it cannot use any of them to walk.

16 A **koala bear's fingerprints** are **so identical** to that of a **human's** that a koala bear can be mistaken for a human in a criminal investigation.

17 **Mickey Mouse** is called "Topolino" in Italy.

18 **Elvis Presley**, a famous American musician and singer, had a middle name, and it was Aron.

19 You **burn** more **calories** eating a stick of **celery** than the stick of celery contains.

20 **Flushing toilets** make up for about 35% of indoor water use.

21 **Milk** from a **camel** does **not curdle**.

22 A **frog** is not able to **swallow** without closing its eyes.

23 Statistically, you share your **birthday** with at least nine million people.

24 You **burn** more **calories** sleeping than you do watching television.

25 A **grape** will **explode** if you put it in the **microwave**.

26 It is actually impossible for a **duck** to **walk** without bobbing its head.

27 **Cows** do not have any upper **teeth**. They only have teeth at the bottom.

28 5% of women and 42% of men do **not wash** their **hands** after going to a public toilet.

29 An **owl** cannot move its **eyes** from side to side. That is why it needs to be able to turn its head all the way around.

30 The **board for Monopoly** was **originally** designed to be a **circle**.

31 For every one human in the world, there are around 200 million **insects**.

32 In the 1800s, there were **teacups** that protected one's **mustache** from getting soaked by tea.

33 More people are **killed** by **falling coconuts** than by **shark attacks**.

34 Cuba has the world's **smallest bird**, called the **bee hummingbird**.

35 There are more **insects** in the world than there are of all the other animals combined.

36 **Crocodiles** will swallow rocks to help them dive deeper into the water.

37 When the toy **yo-yo** was first made, it was originally used as a weapon while hunting animals, not a toy.

38 The lining of your **stomach** blushes the same time your face does.

39 More **money** is printed for **Monopoly** every day than actual money is printed for the U.S. Treasury.

40 It is forbidden to **hypnotize** someone in **public schools** in San Diego.

41 A third of **Americans** will **flush the toilet** while they are still sitting on it.

42 An **emu** cannot walk backward.

43 The average human will **laugh** about ten times a day.

44 The entire **world's population** is 49% women.

45 A **shark** can swim up to 44 miles per hour.

46 **Bats** are the only mammals in the world that can fly.

47 **Bananas** grow while pointing upwards.

48 A **whale** cannot swim backward.

49 **Crocodiles** are more colorblind than dogs.

50 An **armadillo** is able to walk underwater.

51 **Birds** need to **eat** twice their own body weight every day.

52 **Roosters** need to fully extend their necks in order to crow.

53 A **cat's urine** will glow if you put it underneath a blacklight.

54 **Dust** in the **household** is made up of mostly dead skin cells.

55 The word "**level**" is **spelled** the same forwards and backward.

56 You **breathe** about 23,000 times a day.

57 **Ants** need to stretch when they wake up in the morning.

58 Your **forearm** is usually the same **length** as your **foot**.

59 The **cat door** was invented by **Isaac Newton**.

60 There are over 600 rooms inside **Buckingham Palace**.

61 In the country of **Japan**, they have **square watermelons**, which were created to make them easier to stack in the stores.

62 There are more **chickens** in the world than there are people.

63 The **first train** could only travel as fast as five miles per hour.

64 **Apples** contain 25% air, and that is why they float on water.

65 A **flea** is able to jump over 350 times the length of its body.

66 **Porcupines** float in water, but they cannot swim that well.

67 A **turnip** goes green when it gets sunburnt.

68 It is impossible for a **kangaroo** to walk backward.

69 It will only take you an hour to **drive into space**.

70 **Monkeys** go **bald** when they get old, just like humans do.

71 A **woodpecker's tongue** is so long that it can wrap it around its head twice!

72 It is against the **law in England** to stand within about 295 feet of the Queen without wearing socks.

73 A **crocodile** will continuously grow a new set of teeth to replace the old set.

74 Your **nose** and **ears** will carry on **growing** for the rest of your life.

75 A **dog's nose** is exactly like a human's fingerprint; every one is unique.

76 When you roll **dice**, the opposite sides will always add up to seven.

77 In **Australia's Daintree rainforest**, there is a tree that is called the **"Idiot Fruit."**

78 If you give your pet **hamster** a hamster wheel, it will be able to run up to eight miles a night on the wheel.

79 **Jedi** is an actual religion, and there are over 70,000 followers of the **religion in Australia**.

80 Around 90% of people who are **laughing** will laugh even harder when they try to **explain** why they are laughing.

81 Up to 53% of **women** in the world will not leave the house without **makeup** on.

82 A **jellyfish** does not have a **brain**.

83 Around 45% of **Americans** are not aware that the **sun** is a star.

84 A **rhino** only has three **toes** on each of its feet.

85 An **elephant's skeleton** only makes up about 15% of its total body weight.

86 There is a **pill** you can take that will make your **poop smell** like chocolate.

87 There is a fish called "**garfish**" that has **green bones**.

88 80% of the people hit by **lightning** are **men**.

89 In India, some of the **playing cards** are round.

90 An **ant** is able to **lift up** to 50 times its own weight.

91 If a **donkey** has a baby with a **zebra**, that baby is called a "**zonkey**."

92 **Sea lions** are the only animals known that have **rhythm** and can clap to a **beat**.

93 You **cannot smell** anything while you're **asleep**, even a really bad smell.

94 Your **heart stops** beating when you **sneeze**.

95 If you have a **pet bat**, you will not have to worry about **bugs** because they eat 3,000 bugs a night.

96 Before the year 1913, a parent could actually **mail** their **kids** to their grandma's house through the **postal service**.

97 When someone says "**Liar, liar pants on fire**," the correct response is "I don't care, I don't care, I can buy another pair."

98 Some **fish** can actually **cough**.

99 It is physically impossible to **tickle** yourself.

100 The most popular **color** for a **toothbrush** is blue.

01 An **African grey parrot's vocabulary** contains just over 200 words.

02 **Fire** is able to **move** faster going uphill than going downhill.

03 A **crocodile**, like most other lizards, only **grows** as large as its environment allows it to. If it is placed in a small enclosure it will never outgrow that enclosure.

04 There are more **deaths** caused by **hippopotamuses** than any other animal in Africa.

05 The **human brain** contains an average of 78% **water**.

06 There are **more births** in **August** than in any other month.

07 Unless **food mixes** with your **saliva**, you will not be able to **taste** it.

08 There are only four words in the **English language** that end with the letters "d," "o," "u," and "s"; horrendous, tremendous, hazardous, and stupendous.

09 Up to 8% of people on Earth are **born** with an **extra rib**.

10 **Hawaiians** only have 13 letters in their **alphabet**.

11 **Armadillos** always give birth to only four babies at a time.

12 "**Dreamt**" is the only word in the entire **English language** that ends with the letters "mt."

13 **Goldfish** are capable of seeing both **ultraviolet light** and **infrared light**.

14 The **human** body's **smallest bones** are found in the ear.

15 "**Stewardesses**" is the longest word that can be typed using only the left hand.

16 The **original name** for the internet was **ARPANet**, which stands for Advanced Research Projects Agency Network.

17 The **internet** was **originally designed** for use by the U.S. Department of Defense.

18 One **nautical knot out** on the ocean is the same as 1.150 miles on land.

19 "The quick brown fox jumps over the lazy dog" is a **sentence** that uses **all** of the **letters** of the alphabet.

20 There are as many as 26 **bones** in your **foot**. That is one-fourth of your body's bones.

21 If you **add** up all of the numbers from **one to 100**, together it equals 5,050.

22 The number **"one googol"** is basically one followed by 100 zeros.

23 The **largest organ** on the human body is the **skin**.

24 People **throw coins** into the **Trevi Fountain** found in Italy, and the coins are collected for charity.

25 The bone in your throat, known as the **hyoid bone**, is the only bone in your body that is not attached to another bone.

26 Your **tongue heals** faster than any other part of your body.

27 Every day is considered a **holiday** somewhere in the world.

28 "**Laser**" is not just a word; it actually stands for Light Amplification by Stimulated Emission of Radiation.

29 The word "**town**" is the **oldest word** in the English language.

30 The **most sensitive** finger on your hand is your **index finger**.

31 The words "**listen**" and "**silent**" both use the same letters.

32 The **first boats** that were built for sailing were built in **Egypt**.

33 You can fill a matchbox with **gold** and then use the same amount of gold to thinly cover a tennis court.

34 **White cats** born with **blue eyes** are usually also born deaf.

35 A **human body** that weighs approximately 154 pounds will contain about 0.2 milligrams of gold.

36 A **dentist** invented the **electric chair**.

37 The **past tense** of the word **"dare"** is the word **"durst."**

38 **Wind** will not make a **sound** until it blows against something.

39 Humans started **naming hurricanes** and **tropical storms** around the year 1953.

40 **Almond** is a member of the **same family** as a **peach**.

41 **Gold** is known as the only heavy element that will never erode.

42 When you **freeze water**, it **expands** by 9% of its original volume.

43 The only **vitamin** that an **egg** does not contain is vitamin C.

44 You have to climb 1,792 steps to reach the top of the **Eiffel Tower**.

45 There are 2,500,000 **rivets** holding the **Eiffel Tower** together.

46 It takes 50 years for an **oak tree** to start producing **acorns**.

47 The word "**almost**" is the longest English word that is spelled with the letters in alphabetical order.

48 If **human DNA** was stretched out into a single line, it would be able to reach the moon 6,000 times.

49 Your **tongue** is like your fingerprints; it is unique to you.

50 If your body loses 1% of water, you will start to feel **thirsty**.

51 A **dolphin** can reach **speeds** of up to 37 miles per hour.

52 About 10% of your **taste buds** live on your cheeks.

53 New Zealand has about 70 million sheep and only four million people.

54 Wine spoils when it is exposed to light, which is why wine is sold in tinted bottles.

55 Sound is able to travel through water 4.3 times faster than it can travel through the air.

56 600,000 to one are the odds of you being struck by lightning.

57 The most active muscles in your body are the muscles that are in your eyes.

58 You can find vitamin B12 in the rain.

59 Your brain requires at least 25% of the oxygen that you breathe.

60 The reason ice skating rinks will always go counter-clockwise is so that right-handed people, who make up the majority, can grab hold of the railing with their right hand.

61 Your **liver** is used for over 500 different **functions**.

62 A **horse** has 18 more **bones** in its body than humans do.

63 **Hydrogen atoms** are so small that you need two million of them to fully cover a full stop.

64 The **first book** printed in England was about **chess**.

65 The average human body has 59,650 miles of **blood vessels**.

66 Your **stomach acid** is strong enough to dissolve a whole nail.

67 When you are **typing on** a **keyboard**, 56% of the typing is done with your left hand.

68 There are over six million **dust mites** in the average **bed**.

69 A **chameleon** uses its **tongue** to eat, and its tongue is up to twice the length of its body.

70 27% of **food** is **thrown away** in developed countries.

71 When you **recognize** a person's **face**, you are using the **right** side of your **brain** to do so.

72 You **cannot read** in your **dreams** because reading and dreaming actually use two different parts of your brain.

73 A **caterpillar** has more **muscles** than a human does.

74 Every one square inch of your **skin** contains up to 625 **sweat glands**.

75 Your **body temperature** should normally be 99 degrees Fahrenheit.

76 **Gasoline** and **coffee** are the two items that are bought and sold the most throughout the world.

77 When a baby is born, it has 350 **bones**. By the time a child turns five years old, some bones have merged together, giving the child only 206 bones, which is the normal amount for an adult human.

78 In order to make the sound of a **cracking whip**, the tip of the whip must be traveling faster than the speed of sound.

79 The machine that is used to **measure blood** is called a "**sphygmomanometer**."

80 Minus 40 degrees **Fahrenheit** is exactly the same temperature as minus 40 degrees **Celsius**.

81 We only started using **ignition keys** to start **cars** in the year 1949.

82 A **jumbo jet** contains enough **gasoline** in a full tank for a car to drive around the whole world about four times.

83 When **Isaac Newton** first discovered the law of gravity, he was only 23 years old.

84 90% of the **human body** is made up of oxygen, hydrogen, carbon, and nitrogen.

85 If a car is traveling about 50 miles per hour, it will use half of its **fuel** just to overcome the **wind resistance**.

86 The first **lie detector** was invented in the year 1921.

87 **Red light** has a higher wavelength than any other light.

88 **Light** is just electromagnetic radiation.

89 Most **cats** can retract their **claws**; a cheetah is the only cat that cannot.

90 We are not sure, but it is likely that **scissors** were invented in **ancient Egypt**.

91 It's not the air that causes **super glue** to dry; it's **moisture**.

92 7,000 tons of old and worn out **currency** is **shredded** in the United States each year.

93 One ton of **cement** is poured for every woman, man, and child in the world each year.

94 Most of the **vitamin C** in fruit can be found in the skin.

95 The average **human** will **consume** at least 12,000 gallons of **water** and 100 tons of **food** in their lifetime.

96 All letters have one **syllable** except for the letter "**W**" which has three syllables.

97 One **letter** out of every eight letters used when writing or typing is an "**E**."

98 The words "**bump**" and "**assassination**" were invented by **Shakespeare**.

99 There is a phenomenon called "**ghost apples**," in which water freezes around an apple during the colder months, and the apple rots away inside the frozen water. This leaves an apple-shaped ghost-like form of ice.

100 The value of the **number "pi"** was known to only 35 decimal places during the 17th century. Today, it is known to 1.2411 trillion decimal places.

01 **Japan** and **Russia** still have not signed the **peace treaty** that was used to end World War II.

02 The word **"fan"** is short for **"fanatic."**

03 There is a frog called the **"arrow frog"** which contains enough **poison** to kill around 2,200 people or more.

04 An average **panda** will spend up to 12 hours a day just **eating bamboo**.

05 An **elephant's trunk** contains over 40,000 **muscle tendons**.

06 A **camel** has three different **eyelids** to protect its eyes from sand during a storm.

07 A **camel** can also close its **nostrils** during a sandstorm so sand does not get inside them.

08 Lemons that are thinly skinned are the **juiciest lemons**.

09 **Cabbage** is made up of 91% water.

10 **Dry ice** can go from completely solid to a gas state instantly, skipping the liquid stage.

FINAL WORDS

Thank you so much for taking the time to read my book!

I hope you enjoyed reading it as much as enjoyed writing it (which was a whole lot, I might add).

But do you want to know the best thing about this book?

Well, that it doesn't have to end!

You get to keep it forever, which means you can share these facts with everyone you know – so what are you waiting for?

Get reading, get sharing, and get laughing!